CHEMISTRY MADE SIMPLE FOR KIDS VOLUME 1

DISCOVERING THE WONDERS OF MATTER

D SOUGHTOUT

CHEMISTRY MADE SIMPLE FOR KIDS VOLUME 1

Copyright © August 2023 by David Soughtout

All rights reserved. No part of this publication may be reproduced, distributed, or transmitted in any form or by any means, including photocopying, recording, or other electronic or mechanical methods, without the prior written permission of the publisher, except in the case of brief quotations embodied in critical reviews and certain other non-commercial uses permitted by copyright law.

Note To Readers:
The characters portrayed in this book are entirely fictitious. Any resemblance to actual persons, living or dead, or events is purely coincidental.

Thank you for respecting the author's work and supporting creativity and literature. Your purchase of this book allows authors like David Soughtout to continue bringing you exciting and captivating pieces. We hope you enjoy the adventure within these pages!

TABLE OF CONTENTS

About This Book 10

Introduction 12

CHAPTER 1 15

What Is Chemistry? 16

The Wondrous World Of 16
Chemistry

Wonderful Transformations: 18
Chemical Reactions

The Ingredients Of ⋯⋯ 18
Chemistry: Matter States

Chemistry In Everyday Life ⋯⋯ 19

A New Lover Of Chemistry ⋯⋯ 19

Matter-Building Blocks ⋯⋯ 20
Of Everything

Properties Of Matter ⋯⋯ 22

Matter Interactions-The ⋯⋯ 22
Fun Of Chemistry

Importance Of Chemistry ⋯⋯ 24
In Our Everyday Lives

Fascinating Chemistry Facts ⋯⋯ 25

Dancing Raisins ⋯⋯ 25

Exploding Colors ⋯⋯ 25

Glowing Secrets ⋯⋯ 27

Invisible Ink ⋯⋯ 27

Magic Ice Cream ⋯⋯ 27

Super Stretchy Slime ⋯⋯ 29

Fireworks Spectacle ——— 29

Color-Changing ——— 29

Exploding Pops ——— 29

Magic Breath ——— 31

Invisible Air ——— 31

Super Strong Spider Silk ——— 31

Sweet Chemistry ——— 31

Summary ——— 33

Exercise Questions ——— 33

CHAPTER 2 ——— 37

Understanding The Scientific Method ——— 38

What Is The Scientific Method? ——— 38

Conducting Safe Experiment ——— 40

The Scientific Method And Safety ——— 40

Importance Of Safety In Chemistry Experiments ——— 40

Guidelines For Safe Chemistry Experiments	41
Summary	42
Exercise Questions	42
CHAPTER 3	47
Solids, Liquids And Gases	48
Sam The Solid	48
Lucy The Liquid	49
Greg The Gas	49
Changes Of State	51
Summary	54
Exercise Questions	54
CHAPTER 4	58
Mass And Weight	59
Mass And Weight: What Sets Them Apart?	59
Why Are Mass And Weight Essential Properties Of Matter?	61

Volume And Density	63
Volume: The Space Something Takes Up	64
Density: The Secret To Identifying Substances	64
Identifying And Classifying Substances	66
Why Are Volume And Density Essential Properties?	66
Summary	68
Exercise Questions	68
CHAPTER 5	71
Chemical Reactions	72
The Vinegar And Baking Soda Volcano	72
The Classic Mentos And Soda Reaction	75
Acids And Bases	77

Fizzy Lemonade: A Tasty Acid-Base Reaction	77
Colors Of The Rainbow: Acid-Base Indicator	78
Colors And Pigments	80
Chromatography Art: Discover Color Separation	80
Color Blending: The Art Of Mixing Pigments	83
Rainbow Density Column	85
Density In Everyday Life	87
Glossary Of Key Chemistry Terms	88
Chemistry Made Simple: Fun Words To Know	88
Epilogue: The Journey Ahead	91
Exploring The Wonders Of Chemistry	91

WHAT ON EARTH IS NOT CHEMISTRY?

ABOUT THIS BOOK

Welcome to "Chemistry Made Simple for Kids Vol. 1: Discovering the Wonders of Matter"!

Curious minds and young explorers! I am thrilled to introduce you to a fantastic journey through the incredible world of chemistry, designed just for you! Have you ever wondered why the sky is blue, or how your favorite slime magically comes to life? Well, get ready to unlock the secrets of matter and delve into the amazing world of science that surrounds us every day.

Let me share with you the story behind this extraordinary book. One day, while teaching a bright and enthusiastic student like yourself, the idea struck me like a spark! I thought, "Why not create a special book that makes chemistry super easy and exciting for kids?" And that's exactly what I did!

"Chemistry Made Simple for Kids Vol. 1" is a doorway that will open up a world of awe and wonder to you. I know that sometimes science can seem like a mysterious puzzle, but fear not! In this book, I have used kid-friendly language and engaging explanations to ensure you have a blast while learning.

You see, chemistry is all about understanding the tiny building blocks that make up our universe, called atoms and molecules. We will embark on thrilling adventures together as we explore how these small marvels come together to make up everything around us - from the air we breathe to the water we drink.

I promise not to bombard you with complicated terms and boring facts. Instead, we will uncover the mysteries of chemical reactions with fun experiments that you can try at home (with parental supervision, of course!)

Imagine mixing colorful liquids that fizz and bubble or creating your very own volcanoes that erupt! But that's not all - we will also meet some extraordinary scientists who have changed their world with their fantastic discoveries in stories crafted to make your learning experience absolutely fun. I'm sure you will be inspired by these incredible people.

So, whether you dream of becoming a future scientist, a creative inventor, or simply wish to impress your friends with cool chemical tricks, "Chemistry Made Simple for Kids Vol. 1: Discovering the Wonders of Matter" is your perfect companion.

Get ready to uncover the mystery behind everyday stuff and let your imagination soar! Together, we will unravel the secrets of the universe and have a blast doing it. So, grab your lab coat, put on your thinking cap, and let's dive into the colorful of chemistry! Are you excited? I know I am!

Let the adventure begin!

DAVID SOUGHTOUT

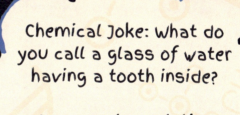

Chemical Joke: What do you call a glass of water having a tooth inside?

A one molar solution

INTRODUCTION

Welcome to the world of chemistry! In this captivating book, we are going to embark on an extraordinary journey to explore the amazing world of molecules, reactions, and matter. Our mission? To make chemistry simple and fun for you!

Chemistry is all around us, it is in the food we eat it is in the air we breathe. It is the science that teaches about the fundamental building blocks of everything in the universe. Even though it might sound complex at first, don't be nervous, for we are about to unlock its secrets and present them to you in the most delightful and understandable way possible.

Imagine being in a magical laboratory where you can mix potions, create colorful explosions, and witness incredible transformations. Well, in a sense, that's exactly what chemists do! They are the modern-day alchemists, combining different substances to create new and exciting wonders.

This book is your very own guide to becoming a young chemist. Together, we will explore the essential concepts of chemistry in an enjoyable and engaging manner. No prior experience is required— only your curiosity and imagination!

Throughout this journey, you will encounter the marvelous world of atoms, the tiny building blocks of matter. These atoms join together to form molecules that make up everything we see and touch.

You will discover how elements and compounds interact, engaging in captivating dances called chemical reactions. Chemistry holds the answers to the mysteries behind the things we see happen everyday.

We will delve into the science behind them and marvel at the beauty of the natural world. Moreover, chemistry extends beyond the boundaries of our planet. By studying the universe, scientists have uncovered the ingredients for stardust, the building blocks of distant celestial bodies. Isn't it fascinating to think that the objects in space, like the moon and planets are all made of stardust?

In this book, we will embrace the spirit of exploration and experimentation. Through safe and exciting hands-on activities and experiments, you will get a chance to be a young scientist right in your own home or classroom.

Remember, making mistakes is an essential part of learning. Even the greatest scientists in history faced challenges and setbacks, but their perseverance led to groundbreaking discoveries that transformed our understanding of the world.

Are you ready to embark on a thrilling adventure of scientific discovery? Let's dive into the world of chemistry, where we will learn, play, and uncover the wonders of this captivating science together.

So, get your lab coat on, put your safety goggles in place, and let's embark on this fascinating journey through The Wonderful World of Chemistry Made Simple for Kids! Let the fun begin!

That the smell of rain has a name? It's called "Petrichor" (pronounced peh-tri-kawr). When raindrops fall on the ground, they can release certain compounds found in rocks, soil, and plants. One of these compounds is called geosmin, which is produced by soil-bacteria. Another compound is released from plant oils. When these compounds are released and mix with the rainwater, they create that unique earthy and pleasant smell we associate with rain. So, the next time you take a deep breath after the rain, you'll know it's the pleasant petrichor scent!

CHAPTER 1

Introduction To Chemistry

What is Chemistry?

In a land far, far away, nestled amid rolling hills and ancient forests, lived a young science enthusiast named Alex. Alex loved experimenting with potions and concoctions to create marvels. However, there was one art he couldn't quite master—the art of chemistry.

One day, while exploring a dusty old library, Alex stumbled upon a dusty, leather-bound book. It had an intriguing title, "The Secrets of Alchemy: Unraveling the Wonders of Chemistry." Curiosity sparked within him, and he opened the book to embark on a magical journey into the world of chemistry.

The Wondrous World Of Chemistry

In the pages of the book, Alex discovered that chemistry is like a dance between the elements of the universe. It is the study of matter—everything around us, be it the shining stars, the lush green forests, or the bubbling potions in his laboratory.

Alex learned that chemistry is all about understanding the tiny building blocks of matter called atoms. These atoms come together to form molecules, just like how he combined ingredients in his laboratory to craft his creations. He discovered that Chemists use elements like oxygen, carbon, and hydrogen to create various substances.

Wonderful Transformations: Chemical Reactions

As Alex delved deeper, he encountered the concept of chemical reactions—a truly exciting phenomenon in chemistry. Chemical reactions are like the grand spectacle of the universe's alchemy. Elements and compounds transform into something entirely new, how amazing!.

He learned that when you mix two or more substances, they sometimes produce a spectacular reaction, releasing light, heat, or fizzles, like his potions when brewed under the full moon. These transformations are like nature's way of creating potions, turning water into ice, or even the sun's rays into vibrant rainbows.

The Ingredients Of Chemistry: Matter States

The book revealed the potions of chemistry—the states of matter: solid, liquid, gas, and even the elusive plasma. Just like his creations in the laboratory, matter can take on different forms depending on its temperature and pressure.

Solid matter is like his crystals, stable and unmoving. Liquid matter flows like the rivers where he swam, while gaseous matter swirls like the winds in the stormy skies. And as for plasma, it's like the ethereal energy that permeates the universe.

Chemistry In Everyday Life

As Alex continued his magical journey, he realized that chemistry is not just confined to ancient books and dusty laboratories. It's everywhere around us, hidden in the most ordinary things.

He learned that the rainbow's vibrant colors are a result of the interaction between light and water droplets which causes it to be reflected through them as rain falls. Even the simplest act of baking a cake or lighting a match is a chemical reaction unfolding before our eyes.

A New Lover Of Chemistry

Alex's journey through the world of chemistry transformed him into a true lover of the subject. Armed with newfound knowledge, he mixed elements, brewed potions, and marveled at the intriguing dance of atoms in every substance.

From that day on, Alex embraced chemistry as a beautiful blend of art and science. Chemistry allows us to understand the mysteries of the universe and create wonders beyond imagination.

Have you ever wondered how bubbles form, why ice melts in the sun, or why your favorite cookies taste so delicious? All these amazing things around us have something in common – they are all part of a fascinating field called chemistry! So, what is chemistry?

Chemistry is the part of science that helps scientists understand everything around us, from the tiniest speck of dust to the shinning stars in the night sky. It is a science that focuses on studying "matter" and its secrets.

Matter is anything that takes up space and has weight, like the air we breathe, the water we drink, and even the colorful crayons we use to paint and create art!

Matter - Building Blocks Of Everything

Imagine you have a giant puzzle, and each piece is like a building block. Well, matter is like those building blocks – everything in the world, including you, is made up of matter! Matter can be tiny, like the invisible air you feel when the wind blows, or it can be huge, like the gigantic mountains that touch the sky. There are three main types of matter – solids, liquids, and gases.

Solids are like those puzzle pieces that fit together tightly and don't change their shape easily. Think of your favorite toy car or a sturdy table; they are both made of solid matter.

Liquids are like water – they flow and take the shape of their container. When you pour yourself a glass of juice, you can see how the liquid fills the glass perfectly.

Gases are the sneakiest of them all! They're sometimes invisible and can spread everywhere. When you blow up a balloon, the air inside it is a gas.

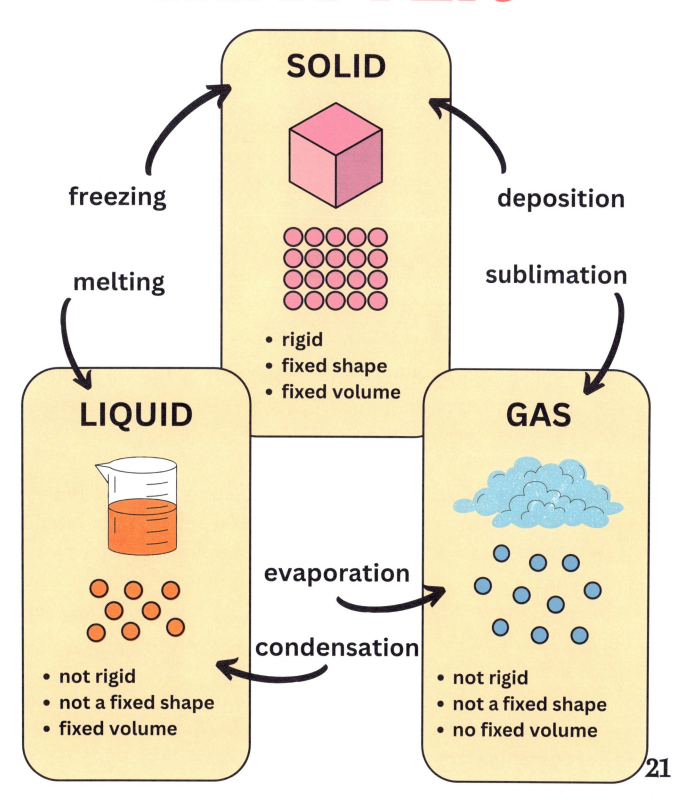

Properties Of Matter

Now that we know about the different types of matter, let's talk about their special properties. Properties are like secret codes that help us identify and understand matter better. For example, a bouncy rubber ball has the property of being flexible, while a shiny metal coin has the property of being smooth. Some properties of matter include:

- Color: The way matter looks.
- Texture: How matter feels, like soft or rough.
- Temperature: How hot or cold matter can be.
- Density: How tightly packed or joined together the matter is in a space.

Matter Interactions - The Fun Of Chemistry

One of the most exciting things about chemistry is the way different types of matter interact with each other. When certain substances come together, they create amazing reactions! Let's explore some fun examples:

- Mixing Colors: Have you ever mixed different colors of paint to create a beautiful masterpiece? When you mix red and yellow paint, you get orange! How about blue and yellow? You get a lovely splash of green.
- Bubbles Galore: Who doesn't love blowing bubbles? The secret behind this bubbly fun is the way soap and air interact to form those shinning spheres.
- Fizz-tastic Soda: When you open a bottle of soda or champagne, you hear a satisfying fizz sound. This is because tiny bubbles of gas are escaping from the liquid!

Importance Of Chemistry In Our Daily Lives

Now, you might be thinking, "Why is chemistry important for me?" Well, chemistry is all around us, making our lives easier, safer, and more fun!

- Medicine: Chemistry helps create medicines that make us feel better when we're sick and keep us healthy!
- Food: Chemistry helps scientist to ensure that our food tastes yummy, stays fresh, and is safe to eat.
- Environment: Chemistry helps scientists protect the environment and keep our air, water, and land clean and healthy. The study of the environment and how to keep it healthy is called Environmental Chemistry.
- Technology: From the devices you use to play games to the cool gadgets adults use, chemistry plays a vital role in making them work.

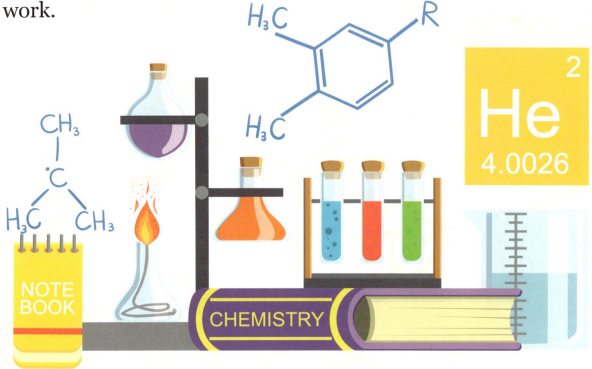

Fascinating Chemistry Facts

Chemistry is like a treasure chest filled with marvelous surprises and exciting mysteries. From colorful explosions to invisible gases, there's so much to learn and explore. So, let's embark on a journey of discovery and uncover some mind-blowing chemistry facts!

Dancing Raisins

Did you know that raisins can dance? It's true! When you drop a few raisins into a glass of soda, they magically start to dance and twirl. Why does this happen? Well, the bubbles in the soda stick to the rough surface of the raisins and carry them to the top. When the bubbles reach the surface, they pop, and the raisins sink back down. This dance goes on and on until all the bubbles disappear!

Exploding Colors:

Imagine a world where colors explode right before your eyes! When you mix two harmless substances called vinegar and baking soda, they create a fantastic chemical reaction. The vinegar and baking soda work together like best friends, and as they mix, they release a gas called carbon dioxide. This gas makes the mixture bubble and fizz, and it even creates a mini-explosion of color if you add a bit of food coloring! It's like a magical rainbow in a glass!

Can you see the raisins rising to the top?

Here's a mini color-explosion.

26

Glowing Secrets

Have you ever wondered why certain things glow in the dark? Well, they have a hidden superpower called "phosphorescence." Phosphorescent things, like glow-in-the-dark stickers or toys, can absorb light when you shine a flashlight on them. Then, when you turn off the lights, they release that stored light in a beautiful glowing display! It's like having a little show of the stars right in your room!

Invisible Ink

Who doesn't love secret messages and spy adventures? With invisible ink, you can become a super cool spy! Lemon juice, milk, or even onion juice can work as invisible ink. Write your message using one of these special liquids, and it won't be visible at first. But when you gently heat the paper, your secret message will magically appear!

Magic Ice Cream

What if I told you that you could make ice cream in just a few minutes using science? Yes, it's true! By mixing cream, sugar, and vanilla together in a bag, and then placing that bag inside another bag filled with ice and salt, you can create a fantastic chemical reaction. The salt makes the ice extra cold, and the cream mixture turns into yummy ice cream right before your eyes! Time to enjoy your tasty homemade treat!

Phosphorescence

Invisible Ink

Ice Cream

Super Stretchy Slime

Who doesn't love playing with slime? But did you know you can make your own slime at home? All you need is some glue and a special mixture called "borax solution." When you mix these two ingredients, they create a super stretchy and gooey slime that you can squish and shape into anything you like!

Fireworks Spectacle

Fireworks are like chemistry's way of throwing a party in the sky! Those dazzling bursts of color and sparkling lights are created by mixing special chemicals inside the fireworks. When the fireworks are set off, these chemicals react and produce beautiful colors, like red from strontium, green from barium, and bright white from magnesium. It's like painting the sky with magic!

Color-Changing

Imagine having a shirt that changes color when you step out into the sun—that's possible with some amazing materials called "thermochromic" and "photochromic" substances. Thermochromic materials change color when they get hot or cold, while photochromic materials change color when exposed to light. It's like wearing a magical outfit that reacts to the world around you!

Exploding Pops

Pop Rocks candy is not just delicious; it's also a chemistry sensation! The tiny popping sounds you hear in your mouth are caused by the candy's secret ingredient – carbon dioxide gas. When Pop Rocks come into contact with your saliva, the carbon dioxide is released, creating those fun popping sensations. It's like having a mini firework show in

 Slime

Fireworks

 Color-changing materials

Pop rock candy

your mouth!

Magic Breath

Ever wondered why winter air feels chilly when you breathe out? It's because of the magic of "condensation." When you breathe out warm air, it meets the cold air outside, and tiny water droplets form, making your breath visible!

Invisible Air

The air around us is like a secret superhero – we can't see it, but it's always there, keeping us alive! Air is made up of different gases, with the most important one being oxygen. When we breathe in, our bodies use the oxygen from the air to stay alive and keep our cells healthy.

Super Strong Spider Silk

Spiders are like little chemists themselves! They spin webs using a special substance called "silk." Spider silk is one of the strongest materials in the world, even stronger than steel! Some scientists are trying to use this incredible silk to make things like bulletproof vests and even artificial limbs. It's like having a superhero material right in nature!

Sweet Chemistry

Who doesn't love sweet treats? The sugar we use to make yummy cookies, cakes, and candies is made from something called "sugar cane." Sugar cane is a tall, grass-like plant that stores lots of sugary juice inside its stems. When the juice is extracted, it's processed into the sugar we know and love. It's like having a natural source of sweetness from the earth!

 ← **Chilly Breath**

Air →

 ← **Spider Silk**

Sugar Cane →

Summary

- Chemistry is a fascinating science that helps us understand everything around us, from tiny particles to the vast universe.
- Matter is the building blocks of everything in the world, and it comes in three main forms: solids, liquids, and gases.
- Matter has special properties that help us identify and understand it better, like color, texture, temperature, and density.
- Chemistry is all about the magical interactions between different substances, creating exciting reactions like mixing colors, blowing bubbles, and fizzy soda.
- Chemistry is essential in our daily lives, as it plays a vital role in creating medicines and ensuring our food is safe and delicious.

Exercise Questions

- What is chemistry, and what does it help us understand?

- Name the three main forms of matter and give an example of each.

- What are properties of matter, and why are they important?

- Can you give an example of an interaction between substances?

- Why is chemistry important for our daily lives? Give at least two examples.

Did you know that there's a substance that can change its state from solid to gas without becoming a liquid first? It's called "dry ice"! Dry ice is actually solid carbon dioxide (CO2) which is the same gas that we exhale when we breathe! When carbon dioxide is super cold, about -78.5 degrees Celsius (-109.3 degrees Fahrenheit), it changes directly from a solid to a gas in a process called "sublimation."

One of the coolest things about dry ice is that it doesn't melt like regular ice. Instead of turning into a liquid, it goes from a solid straight to a gas, creating a spooky fog-like effect. That's why you might have seen it used in Halloween decorations or in special effects for movies and stage performances.

But be careful, because dry ice is extremely cold, it can cause frostbite if you touch it with your bare hands. So, if you ever encounter dry ice, make sure to handle it with thick gloves or use it under adult supervision.

Isn't it fascinating how a simple substance like carbon dioxide can do something so extraordinary? Chemistry is full of surprising phenomena like this that can be both fun and educational!

CHAPTER 2

Understanding The Scientific Method

Understanding The Scientific Method

Have you ever wondered how scientists make incredible discoveries and find answers to all sorts of questions? Well, they use a special tool called the Scientific Method! It's like a treasure map that helps them explore the world around us and solve problems. In this chapter, we'll learn all about the Scientific Method and how it helps us understand the wonders of chemistry in a way that's easy to understand.

What Is The Scientific Method?

The Scientific Method is a step-by-step process that scientists use to find answers and learn new things about the world. It's like a recipe for discovering amazing facts! This method helps scientists figure out how things work, why they happen, and what we can do with this knowledge.

- **Step 1: Ask a Question**

Everything starts with a question. Scientists are naturally curious people who wonder about the world and ask lots of questions. For example, they might ask, "Why do apples fall from trees?" or "What happens when we mix baking soda and vinegar?"

- **Step 2: Do Some Research**

Once scientists have a question, they become like detectives! They search for clues and gather information from books, websites, and other scientists' work. This helps them understand what others have already discovered about their question.

- **Step 3: Make a Hypothesis**

A hypothesis is like a smart guess. Scientists use all the information they found to make an educated prediction about the answer to their question. It's like saying, "I think this will happen because of these reasons."

- **Step 4: Conduct an Experiment**

This step is where the real fun begins! Scientists create an experiment to test their hypothesis. They set up everything carefully and perform the experiment multiple times to make sure the results are reliable. It's like being a mad scientist in a lab, but without the crazy hair!

- **Step 5: Collect Data**

During the experiment, scientists take notes and collect data, which means they write down what happens and what they observe. It's like keeping a secret journal of all the important stuff!

- **Step 6: Analyze the Results**

With all the data in hand, scientists analyze the information to see if their hypothesis was right or wrong. They look for patterns and draw conclusions from the data they collected.

- **Step 7: Draw a Conclusion**

Now, it's time to answer the question based on the results of the experiment. If the hypothesis was correct, the scientist will explain why and share what they learned. If the hypothesis was wrong, that's okay too! Science isn't about being right all the time; it's about learning from mistakes and making new discoveries.

- **Step 8: Share Your Findings**

Scientists love to share their discoveries with the world! They write papers, make presentations, and sometimes even make cool videos to explain what they found. By sharing their work, they help other scientists learn and build on their ideas.

Conducting Safe Experiment

Just like superheroes, scientists have a special power too - the ability to conduct exciting experiments! However, with great power comes great responsibility. That's why safety is SUPER important when it comes to conducting chemistry experiments. You're about to learn about the importance of safety in science and discover some simple guidelines to keep young scientists like you safe and sound while exploring the wonders of chemistry!

The Scientific Method And Safety

Remember how we talked about the Scientific Method earlier? Well, safety is a crucial ingredient in this recipe of science. Scientists follow safety guidelines to protect themselves and others while performing experiments. Just like a superhero needs a shield to stay safe, scientists need safety rules to keep them out of harm's way!

Importance Of Safety In Chemistry Experiments

Chemistry is like a fantastic cooking show - you mix different ingredients and create amazing recipes! But just like a chef who practices a lot before performing, scientists need to practice safety measures to avoid accidents. Here are some reasons why safety is essential in chemistry experiments:

- **Prevent Accidents:** Safety rules are like a superhero's shield - they protect you from harm. Accidents can happen when chemicals are handled improperly, so following safety guidelines is crucial to avoid injuries.

- **Protect the Environment:** Just like superheroes save the planet in movies, scientists must also protect the environment. Some chemicals can harm nature, so proper disposal and handling are vital to keep the world safe and clean.
- **Keep Others Safe:** Scientists often work in teams, just like superheroes fighting together against villains. Safety rules ensure that everyone in the lab or at home stays safe during experiments.

Guidelines For Safe Chemistry Experiments

Now, let's learn some simple safety guidelines that every young scientist should follow while conducting chemistry experiments:

- **Adult Supervision:** Always have an adult superhero (like a teacher or a parent) with you during experiments. They will guide you and ensure everything goes smoothly.
- **Read and Follow Instructions:** Just like superheroes follow their mission plans, read and understand the experiment instructions carefully before starting. Don't skip any steps!
- **Wear Safety Gear:** Just like how superheroes wear special suits for protection, you should wear safety gear too! Lab coats, safety goggles, and gloves will keep you safe from chemicals.
- **Use the Right Equipment:** Make sure to use the correct tools and equipment for your experiment. Using the wrong equipment can lead to unexpected reactions!
- **Keep the Area Clean:** Superheroes don't like messes, and neither do scientists! Keep your workspace tidy to avoid accidents and mix-ups.
- **Handle Chemicals Carefully:** Treat chemicals like precious gems. Always pour them carefully, and never touch or taste them

unless your experiment specifically says it's safe to do so.
- **Use Small Quantities:** Just like superheroes don't use all their powers at once, use small quantities of chemicals during experiments. This way, if something goes wrong, the impact will be minimal.
- **No Eating or Drinking:** Chemistry experiments are not like snack time! Never eat or drink anything while conducting an experiment, even if you think it's safe.

Summary

- The Scientific Method is a step-by-step process that scientists use to explore the world, find answers, and make amazing discoveries in a systematic way.
- Safety is a crucial aspect of conducting chemistry experiments to prevent accidents, protect the environment, and ensure the well-being of scientists and others involved.
- Guidelines for safe chemistry experiments include having adult supervision, reading and following instructions carefully, wearing safety gear, using the right equipment, keeping the workspace clean, handling chemicals with care, using small quantities, and refraining from eating or drinking during experiments.

Exercise Questions

- What is the Scientific Method, and how does it help scientists in their exploration and discoveries?

_____

_____

_____

- Why is safety important in conducting chemistry experiments? Provide at least two reasons.

  _____

  _____

  _____

- List three guidelines to follow for safe chemistry experiments.

  _____

  _____

  _____

  _____

- Why should young scientists always have an adult supervising their experiments?

  _____

  _____

- True or False: Scientists should treat chemicals with care and avoid touching or tasting them unless stated otherwise in the experiment instructions.

  _____

- What is the importance of using small quantities of chemicals during experiments?

  _____

  _____

- Why is it essential to keep the workspace clean during chemistry experiments?

  _____

  _____

- Name three pieces of safety gear that scientists should wear while conducting experiments.

  _____

  _____

  _____

- How can scientists protect the environment during their chemistry experiments?

  _____

  _____

- Why is it important to read and understand the experiment instructions carefully before starting an experiment?

  _____

  _____

  _____

Did you know that the color of a flame can tell us what elements are present in a material? When you see a flame, it might appear to be a simple orange or yellow color, but if you look closely, you'll notice that some flames can be different colors. For example, a candle flame is typically yellow, while a Bunsen burner flame can be blue.

The color of a flame is determined by the energy released when certain elements burn. When an element or a compound is heated, the electrons in its atoms get excited and jump to higher energy levels. As they return to their original positions, they release energy in the form of light, and the color of that light depends on the element.

For instance, when sodium burns, it produces a bright yellow flame. Copper gives off a greenish-blue flame, while lithium burns with a beautiful crimson-red color.

This property is so reliable that scientists and firefighters use it to identify unknown chemicals in fires. They use special equipment to analyze the flame's color and determine which elements are present in the burning material. It's like chemistry magic in action!

Next time you see a flame, pay attention to its color. Who knows, you might be witnessing the unique colors of different elements right before your eyes!

CHAPTER 3
STATES OF MATTER

Solids, Liquids, And Gases

Once upon a time, in a far-off land, there was a curious young explorer named Emma. One sunny day, while taking a nap, she had a dream, where she found herself in a land filled with wonders. This place was like no other - the Land of Matter!

In this extraordinary dream, Emma encountered three fascinating characters: Sam the Solid, Lucy the Liquid, and Greg the Gas. Each of them was a unique representation of the three main states of matter: solids, liquids, and gases.

Sam The Solid

As Emma followed a winding path, she saw a friendly figure made of colorful building blocks, standing tall and strong. It was Sam, the Solid! He taught Emma all about solids, which are substances with a fixed shape and volume. Sam explained that solids are like these building blocks, tightly packed together, and they don't like to move around much. When you try to squish a solid, it resists being compressed and retains its shape. Just like a block tower, solids stay in one place unless something pushes or pulls them. Some examples of solids are ice, rocks, and even the wooden floor Emma was standing on.

Lucy The Liquid

Further along the path, Emma encountered a shinning figure that seemed to flow like a river. It was Lucy, the Liquid! She happily welcomed Emma and taught her all about liquids, which take the shape of their container and have a fixed volume.

Lucy explained that liquids are like the river, flowing smoothly and filling any space they are poured into. They can be poured from one container to another and can take various shapes, adapting to the shape of their container. When you try to compress a liquid, it doesn't resist as much as a solid, but it still has a fixed volume. Examples of liquids include water, juice, and even the refreshing lemonade Emma enjoyed in the Land of Matter.

Greg The Gas

As Emma explored even further, she noticed a playful figure floating around like a cloud. It was Greg, the Gas! He was full of energy and taught Emma all about gases, which have neither a fixed shape nor volume. Greg explained that gases are like the free-spirited clouds that can expand and fill any available space. They don't have a definite shape or volume, and they can be compressed easily. When you heat a gas, it gains energy and expands; conversely, cooling it causes it to condense into a liquid or even a solid. Examples of gases are the air we breathe, steam, and the invisible gases that filled the Land of Matter.

In the Land of Matter, Emma saw that substances could transition from one state to another. When Sam the Solid was heated, he turned into Lucy the Liquid. When Lucy was further heated, she transformed

into Greg the Gas. And when Greg was cooled down, he returned to his liquid and solid forms. Back in the real world, when Emma woke up, she couldn't shake off the incredible adventure she had just experienced. She realized that the Land of Matter had taught her a valuable lesson about the states of matter.

Matter exists in three main states: solids, liquids, and gases. Solids have a fixed shape and volume, liquids take the shape of their container but have a fixed volume, and gases have neither a fixed shape nor volume. Understanding these states of matter helps us make sense of the world around us, from the food we eat to the water we drink and then to the air we breathe. So, the next time you see a solid block, pour a liquid into a glass, or feel the air on your skin, remember the amazing adventures in the Land of Matter and the fascinating states that matter can take!

Changes Of State

The Magic of Changes: When Matter Gets a Makeover!

Have you ever wondered how a solid ice cube turns into a puddle of water on a hot summer day? Or why your breath sometimes forms a mist on chilly mornings? Well, get ready for some chemistry because we're going to uncover the world of "Changes of State"!

Imagine you have a special substance called "Matter Transformer." That can transform everyday substances like water, ice, and even steam into different states. Let's see what happens when we use this imaginary trusty substance of ours!

- **Mighty Melting:** Take an ice cube from the freezer and place it on a sunny windowsill. As you sprinkle the "Matter Transformer" on the ice cube, get ready to be amazed! The ice starts to tremble and shake. Slowly but surely, it begins to transform into a delightful liquid. Voilà! You've just witnessed the marvelous process of melting!

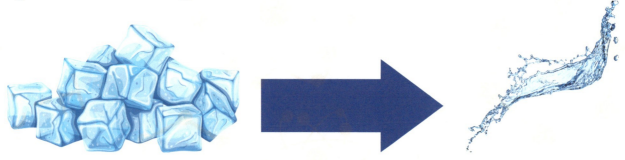

Melting happens when a solid (like ice) soaks up some warmth and becomes a liquid (like water). This usually occurs when the temperature rises above the freezing point of the substance. It's like the ice can't resist the sunshine's warm hug and decides to become a free-flowing liquid to enjoy the sunny party!

- **Fantastic Freezing:** Now, let's do the opposite! Take that bowl of water and put it in the freezer. Sprinkle some "Matter Transformer" on it and watch closely. The once free-flowing water begins to shiver and quiver. Slowly, it transforms back into a rock-hard ice cube. Ta-da! This process is called freezing! Freezing is like magic in reverse. When a liquid (like water) gets chilly and the temperature drops below its freezing point, it decides to gather together and form a solid (like ice). It's like the water likes to huddle close, forming beautiful ice crystals to stay warm and cozy!

- **Epic Evaporation:** Now, let's take our experiment to a different level. Fill a bowl with water and place it in the sunshine. As you sprinkle the "Matter Transformer," something extraordinary happens! The water slowly starts to disappear into thin air. This phenomenon is called evaporation! Evaporation is like a water adventure. When a liquid (like water) gets warm enough, it starts to rise up and escape into the air as an invisible vapor (like steam). It's like the water wants to explore the sky and join the clouds for an exciting adventure!

- **Captivating Condensation:** For our final trick, let's reverse the spell of evaporation. Take a mirror or a window and breathe on it to create some fog. Now, sprinkle the "Matter Transformer" on the foggy surface and wait for the enchantment! The fog begins to shrink and gather together, forming tiny droplets of water. Bravo! You've just witnessed the magical process of condensation!

Condensation is like a secret reunion of friends. When the invisible vapor (like steam) cools down, it changes back into tiny water droplets (like fog or dew). It's like the steam can't resist coming back together, forming tiny droplets that love to play hide-and-seek with us!

And there you have it, the marvelous world of "Changes of State"! With our trusty "Matter Magic Elixir," we can make matter dance and transform into different states. So, the next time you see a melting ice cream, enjoy a freezing snowball fight, witness the mysterious fog, or feel the steam from a hot cup of cocoa, remember the chemistry of changes happening all around us! Chemistry is full of wonders, and you're now a true Matter Genius!

Summary

- The states of matter: solids, liquids, and gases.
- Solids have a fixed shape and volume, like colorful building blocks, and they resist being compressed.
- Liquids take the shape of their container and have a fixed volume, flowing smoothly like a river.
- Gases have neither a fixed shape nor volume, expanding to fill any space like playful clouds.
- Matter can change from one state to another through magical processes: melting, freezing, evaporation, and condensation.

Exercise Questions

- How does a solid differ from a liquid in terms of shape and volume?

  _____

  _____

- Can you give an example of a solid, a liquid, and a gas from your everyday life activities?

  _____

  _____

- What happens during melting? Can you describe a real-life example of melting?

  _____

  _____

  _____

  _____

- How is freezing different from melting?

  _____

  _____

- Imagine you have a bowl of water on a sunny day. What do you think will happen to the water over time, and why?

  _____

  _____

- Can you explain the process of evaporation? Mention something wet that dries up over time due to evaporation.

  _____

  _____

- What is condensation, and how is it related to evaporation? How can you create condensation on a mirror or window?

  _____

  _____

- Can you think of a fun experiment to show how water can change states? Describe the steps and what you expect to happen.

_____
_____
_____
_____
_____
_____
_____
_____

Did you know that there's a liquid that can "eat" right through metal? It's called "aqua regia," which is Latin for "royal water"!

Aqua regia is a powerful and highly corrosive mixture of two acids: hydrochloric acid (HCl) and nitric acid (HNO_3). When combined, these two acids create a solution that can dissolve precious metals like gold and platinum, as well as other metals like copper and silver.

This special ability makes aqua regia essential in some scientific processes and even used in the recovery of precious metals from old electronic devices or jewelry.

Interestingly, aqua regia was first used by alchemists in their quest to turn base metals into gold. While they didn't succeed in that goal, they did discover this extraordinary corrosive mixture that still has important applications in chemistry today.

Remember, aqua regia is incredibly powerful and dangerous to handle, so it should only be used by trained professionals in controlled laboratory settings.

Isn't it amazing how something as simple as a mixture of acids can have such a dramatic effect on metals?

CHAPTER 4
PROPERTIES OF MATTER

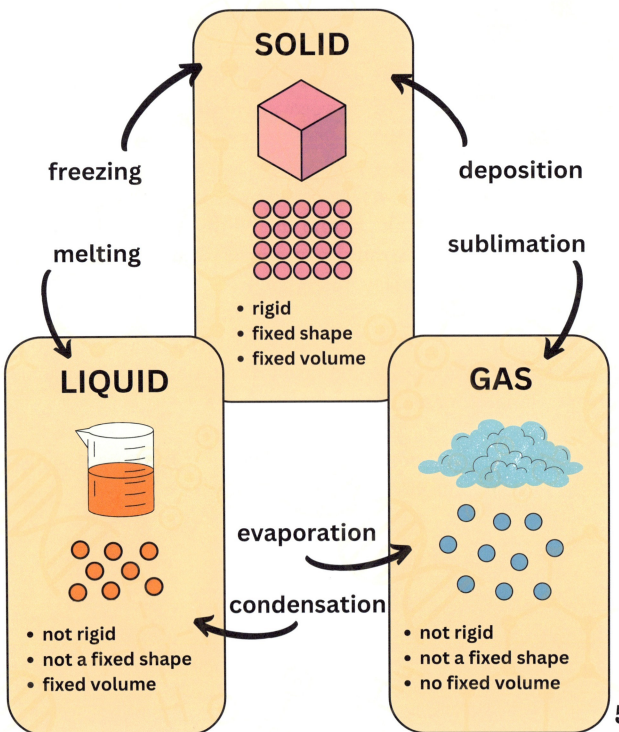

Mass And Weight

Once upon a time, in the town of Scientopia, lived a curious young boy named Tim. Tim loved exploring the world around him and was always eager to learn new things. One sunny day, while Tim was playing in the park, he encountered a peculiar creature called Graviton, who introduced himself as the Guardian of Gravity.

Graviton, a friendly being with a round body and a smiling face, explained that he had a unique ability to control the force that makes everything on Earth stay grounded - gravity. Tim was amazed by this revelation, and he decided to accompany Graviton on an extraordinary journey to discover the fantastic properties of matter.

Mass And Weight: What Sets Them Apart?

Graviton and Tim set off on their adventure, soaring through the skies to learn about the properties of matter. The first concept they encountered was "mass." Graviton explained that mass is the amount of stuff, or matter, something is made of. Everything around us, whether it's a tiny pebble or a massive elephant, has mass. The more matter an object has, the greater its mass!

Tim and Graviton landed on a space station orbiting Earth, where they met some space explorers. The space explorers showed them an exciting experiment. They had two identical-looking backpacks, but one was filled with feathers, and the other had rocks inside. Even though the backpacks looked the same, the one with rocks was much heavier!

Graviton then clarified the difference between mass and weight. He said, "Tim, my young friend, while mass tells us how much stuff is in an object, weight depends on both mass and gravity. The force of gravity pulls objects towards Earth's center. So, the rocks in the backpack felt heavier because they experienced more pull from the gravitational force than the feathers."

Tim was quick to understand. He realized that the same object could weigh differently on Earth and on other planets because gravity is not the same everywhere.

Why Are Mass and Weight Essential Properties of Matter?

As Tim and Graviton continued their journey, they encountered a group of playful aliens who were bouncing on a trampoline. Tim was fascinated to see how high or low they could jump based on their mass. The lighter aliens bounced higher, while the heavier ones didn't reach as high.

Graviton explained that mass and weight are essential properties of matter because they affect how objects interact with each other and with the world around them. Without mass, nothing would exist! We wouldn't have the sun, the moon, or even ourselves. It is mass that gives objects substance and makes them real. Weight is equally important because it helps us understand how objects behave under gravity's influence. This knowledge is crucial for architects, engineers, and scientists who design structures and build things that need to withstand gravity's pull. Tim's Adventure Continues...

Just like this boy, gravity pulls everything towards the earth.

The greater the mass of an object, the greater the gravitational force it experiences. That force is called "weight"

Gravity

Tim was thrilled to have learned so much about mass and weight during his adventure with Graviton. As they bid farewell to the friendly aliens and returned to Scientopia, Tim knew he had discovered something extraordinary. From that day on, Tim became the town's resident science enthusiast, sharing his adventures and knowledge with all the kids in the neighborhood. He would often tell stories about the marvelous Guardian of Gravity, Graviton, and his captivating journey through the properties of matter.

So, the next time you wonder why things fall to the ground or why some objects are heavier than others, remember the adventures of Tim and Graviton. Understanding mass and weight might just be the first step on your own exciting journey into the intriguing world of science!

Volume And Density

In the land of Wonderia, lived a young explorer named Lily. Lily had an insatiable curiosity about the world and loved to discover new things. One day, as she was wandering in the woods, she stumbled upon a magical creature named Densito, the Density Guardian. Densito, a cheerful being with a shining aura, possessed an extraordinary ability to understand the compactness of everything around him. Intrigued by this power, Lily decided to accompany Densito on an extraordinary voyage to unravel the captivating properties of volume and density.

Volume: The Space Something Takes Up

Lily and Densito embarked on their adventure, floating through the skies to learn about the fascinating properties of matter. The first concept they encountered was "volume." Densito explained that volume is the amount of space something occupies. It's like how much room an object takes up. He showed Lily a small, round bottle and a large, square box, both filled with water. Though the two containers looked different, they held the same amount of water because their volume was the same.

The magical duo decided to test this concept further by pouring the water from the bottle into a tall, skinny glass. Despite the different shapes, the water level stayed the same because the volume remained constant.

Density: The Secret To Identifying Substances

As Lily and Densito continued their journey, they arrived at a cave filled with sparkling crystals. Densito showed Lily a brilliant crystal and a dull stone, both the same size. He asked her to guess which one was more dense, and Lily chose the crystal because it looked shinier. Densito then revealed the secret behind density. He said, "Lily, my adventurous friend, density tells us how much stuff, or matter, is packed into a given volume. The crystal is denser than the stone because it has more matter packed into the same space." To help Lily understand better, Densito led her to a grove of trees.

In this case, the volumes of both the box and the water bottle are the same. This is because the amount of spaces they occupy are the same, although they appear different.

The shining stone is more dense than the dull one, because it has more matter packed into the space it occupies. Remember, volume is the amount of space something occupies.

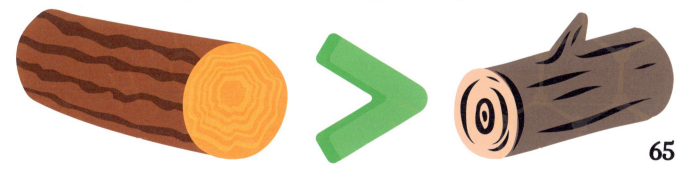

He pointed out that a small, heavy log could be denser than a larger, lighter one because the small log contained more matter in the same volume.

Identifying And Classifying Substances

Lily was thrilled to learn how volume and density helped identify and classify substances. Densito showed her how objects with low density ike balloons filled with air, floated effortlessly, while objects with higher density, like rocks, sank in water. The duo continued their adventure, encountering various materials like feathers, steel, and wood. Lily marveled at how their different densities explained their behavior in different situations. She realized that scientists and engineers use density to identify materials, design objects, and even help solve mysteries.

Why Are Volume And Density Essential Properties?

Lily's voyage with Densito taught her that volume and density are essential properties of matter because they allow us to understand and describe the physical world. By knowing an object's volume, we can figure out how much space it occupies, which is crucial for designing containers and buildings. Density, on the other hand, helps us classify substances based on their compactness. It provides valuable information for various industries, such as construction, transportation, and even cooking! For example, chefs use the density of different ingredients to create mouthwatering recipes. Lily's Incredible Journey Continues...

Object	Volume	Density
	High	Very Low
	Very low	Very High
	Low	High
	Low	Low
	Very High	Moderate

As Lily and Densito bid farewell to the sparkling crystals and the grove of trees, she knew she had gained an extraordinary understanding of volume and density. Back in Wonderia, she shared her captivating adventure with all her friends, Becoming the town's knowledge-hungry explorer. So, the next time you wonder why some things float and others sink, or how we identify different materials, remember the fantastic journey of Lily and Densito.

Summary

- The properties of matter include "mass," which is the amount of stuff in an object, and "weight," which depends on both mass and gravity.
- Mass makes everything exist, and weight helps objects behave under gravity's pull, making them essential properties of matter.
- Another one is "volume," which is the space something occupies, and "density," the compactness of matter in a given volume.
- Density helps identify and classify substances based on their
- compactness. These properties are crucial for designing structures,
- understanding materials, and even cooking delicious recipes.

Exercise Questions

- What is mass, and why is it an essential property of matter?

  _____

  _____

  _____

- Explain the difference between mass and weight.

  _____

  _____

- Why did the rocks in the backpack feel heavier than the feathers?

- How does gravity influence the weight of an object?

- What is volume, and how is it different from mass?

- Give an example of two different objects that have the same volume.

- How does density help us identify and classify substances?

- Why do some objects float in water while others sink?

Did you know that the element "phosphorus" was discovered by accident in the 17th century?

Back in 1669, a German alchemist named Hennig Brand was on a quest to find the Philosopher's Stone, a mythical substance believed to turn base metals into gold and grant eternal life. During his experiments, he collected and boiled down large amounts of urine, hoping to extract the secret ingredient that would lead to his desired discoveries.

As he heated the urine, a waxy substance formed and glowed in the dark with a faint greenish light. Though he didn't find the Philosopher's Stone, Hennig Brand stumbled upon something fascinating and groundbreaking – he had discovered phosphorus!

Phosphorus is a highly reactive and essential element found in our bones and in many of the foods we eat. Thanks to Hennig Brand's accidental discovery, we now know more about this important element and how it contributes to the world of chemistry and biology. So, sometimes, great discoveries can happen by chance!

CHAPTER 5

FUN EXPERIMENTS

Chemical Reactions

Science is a blast when you get to see exciting chemical reactions happen right before your eyes! Chemical reactions occur when different substances mix together and create something entirely new. We're going to explore some fun experiments that are safe and perfect for you to try out. So put on your lab coat and safety goggles, and let's get experimenting!

The Vinegar And Baking Soda Volcano

The vinegar and baking soda volcano is a classic and thrilling experiment that will leave you in awe! Here's what you need:

An empty plastic bottle (a small water bottle will work)
- Baking soda
- Vinegar
- Funnel (optional but helpful)
- Red food coloring (optional)

Instructions:
- Find a safe outdoor space to conduct the experiment.
- Using a funnel, pour a generous amount of baking soda into the plastic bottle (about 2-3 tablespoons).
- If you want to add some drama to your volcano, you can add a few drops of red food coloring to the baking soda.
- Slowly pour vinegar into the bottle, and watch as the magic happens! The vinegar will react with the baking soda, creating carbon dioxide gas. The gas will bubble up and push the mixture out of the bottle, mimicking a volcanic eruption.

Step 1 →

Step 2 →

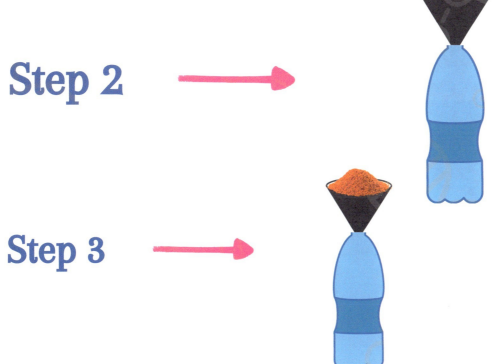

Step 3 →

73

Step 4 →

Safety Note: Although vinegar and baking soda are safe household items, it's essential to perform this experiment under adult supervision. Also, avoid inhaling the gas that is produced during the reaction.

The Classic Mentos And Soda Reaction

Prepare yourself for a fizzy adventure with the Mentos and soda experiment! Here's what you need:
- A roll of Mentos candies (mint flavor works best)
- A 2-liter bottle of soda (diet soda works better as it produces a more vibrant reaction)
- An open outdoor space or a big container to catch the mess

Instructions:
- Again, find a safe outdoor area for the experiment or use a large container meant for catching the soda overflow.
- Open the bottle of soda and place it on a flat surface.
- Quickly drop the entire roll of Mentos candies into the soda bottle and step back!
- The Mentos candies contain tiny pores that help release carbon dioxide gas from the soda at an incredibly fast rate, creating an explosive soda geyser.

Safety Note: The soda geyser can shoot high into the air, so make sure to stand back and avoid getting hit by the soda. This experiment should only be performed with adult supervision. Chemical reactions are fascinating and are a whole lot of fun to explore. The vinegar and baking soda volcano and the Mentos and soda reaction are just two examples of how science can surprise and delight us.

Acids And Bases

Have you ever wondered what makes things taste sour or feel slippery? Well, it's all about acids and bases! Acids are like the sour superheroes, while bases are the slippery sidekicks. We're going to have a blast exploring these concepts through fun experiments, like making fizzy lemonade using citric acid and baking soda. So put on your scientist hat and let's dive into the world of acids and bases!

Fizzy Lemonade: A Tasty Acid-Base Reaction

Prepare to quench your thirst with a fizzy, lemony delight! For this experiment, we'll use two superhero ingredients: citric acid and baking soda.

What you'll Need:
- Fresh lemon or lemon juice
- Water
- Sugar (optional for sweetness)
- Baking soda
- A tall glass or cup
- A spoon for stirring

Instructions:
- Start by squeezing fresh lemon juice into a tall glass or cup. If you don't have fresh lemons, you can use store-bought lemon juice.
- Add a small amount of water to the lemon juice to dilute it and make it less sour. You can also add some sugar if you want your lemonade to be sweeter.
- Now comes the exciting part! Add a tiny amount of baking soda to the lemonade mixture and give it a good stir.

- Watch as the magic happens! The citric acid in the lemon juice and the baking soda will react, producing bubbles of carbon dioxide gas. This will make your lemonade fizzy and exciting!
- Take a sip and enjoy your homemade fizzy lemonade!

Colors Of The Rainbow: Acid-Base Indicator

Discover the colorful side of acids and bases with this fun experiment using red cabbage as an indicator!

What you'll Need:
- Red cabbage
- Water
- Strainer
- Clear containers or glasses
- Lemon juice or vinegar (acidic solution)
- Baking soda dissolved in water (basic solution)

Instructions:
- Cut a few leaves of red cabbage into small pieces and put them in a pot.
- Add enough water to cover the cabbage leaves and bring it to a boil. Let it simmer for about 10 minutes.
- Once the water turns purple, strain out the cabbage leaves, and let the purple liquid cool down. Pour the purple liquid into clear containers or glasses. Also pour your acidic and basic solutions into separate containers.
- Now, put a few drops of lemon juice or vinegar to a separate container, then add a few drops of the cabbage juice. Watch the liquid turn pink or red. Lemon juice and vinegar are acidic, and they change the color of the indicator to show us they are acids.

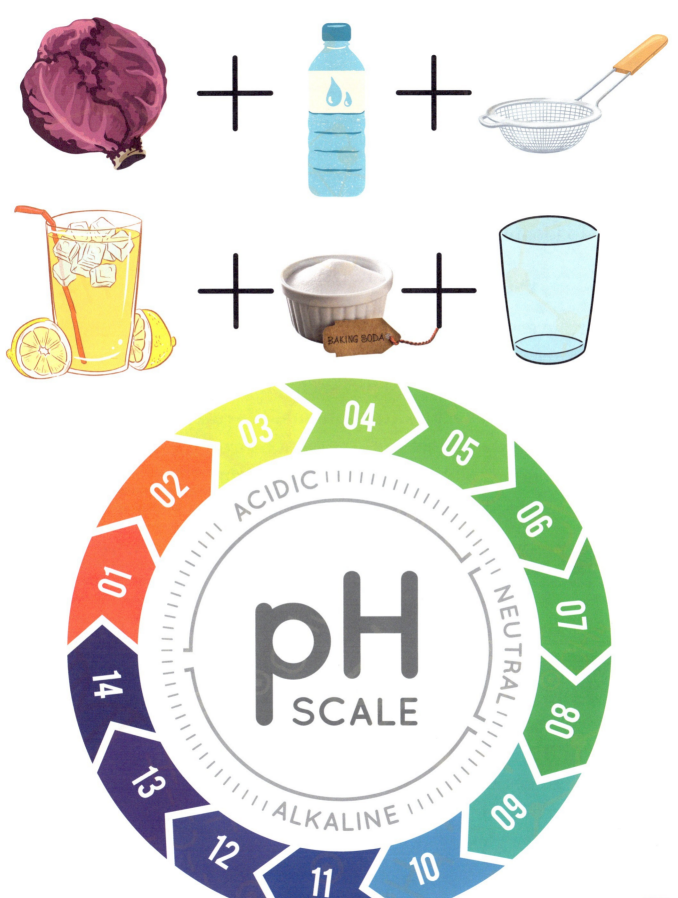

- In another container, add a few drops of baking soda dissolved in water.
- Add a few drops of the cabbage juice to it and observe how the liquid turns green or blue. Baking soda is basic and changes the color of the indicator to show it is a base. Acids and bases are all around us, and they make science a whole lot of fun! Through these exciting experiments, we've learned about fizzy reactions and how to identify acids and bases using colorful indicators.

Colors And Pigments

Colors are everywhere around us, making our world a vibrant and exciting place. Have you ever wondered how different colors are created and why some colors seem to blend into each other effortlessly? Well, it's all about pigments! We're going to dive into the fascinating world of colors and pigments through a fun experiment called chromatography art using colored markers. So, grab your markers and let's create some colorful masterpieces!

Chromatography Art: Discover Color Separation

Chromatography is a super cool scientific technique that helps us separate and explore the different pigments that make up the colors in our markers. Get ready to create beautiful designs!

What you'll Need:
- White coffee filters or filter paper (cut into strips or circles)
- A variety of colored markers
- Clear cups or glasses
- Water
- Pipettes or droppers (optional but helpful)

Instructions:
- Start by setting up your workspace. Place the clear cups or glasses in a row, and label each cup with the color of the marker you'll be using.
- Take a coffee filter or filter paper and use the colored markers to draw small dots or lines near the bottom edge of the paper. Use as many colors as you like and get creative with your designs!
- Pour a small amount of water into each cup, just enough to cover the bottom. The water level should be below the marker-drawn dots or lines.
- Carefully place each coffee filter strip into the corresponding cup, ensuring that the marker-drawn part is just above the water without touching it.
- Now, sit back and watch the experiment unfold happen! As the water slowly travels up the coffee filter, it will carry the pigments from the marker with it. You'll observe the colors separating and creating beautiful patterns on the filter paper.
- Once the water has reached the top of the coffee filter or when you're happy with the design, carefully remove the filter paper and let it dry.
- Your chromatography art is complete! Admire the vibrant colors and unique patterns you've created.

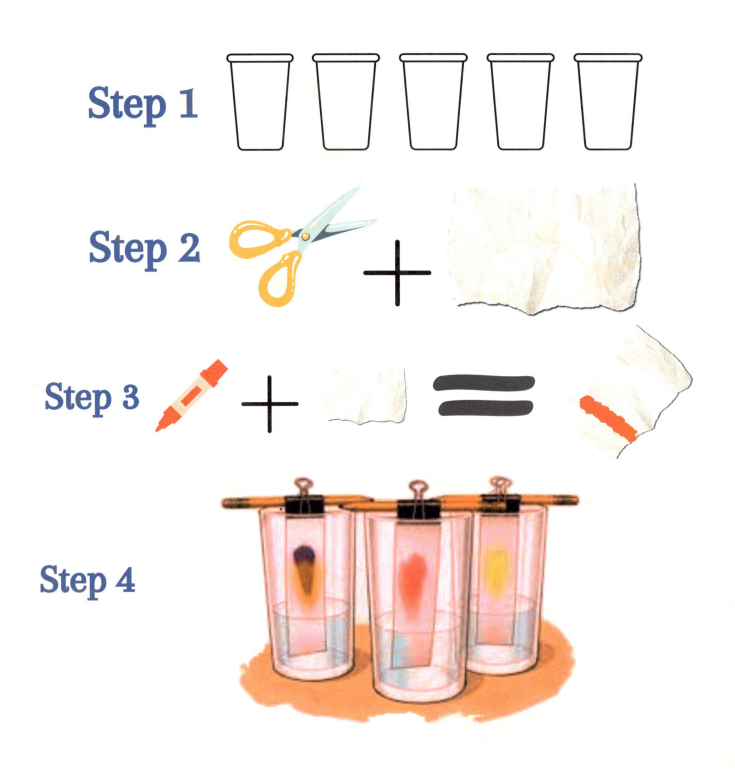

Color Blending: The Art Of Mixing Pigments

Now that you've experienced the excitement of chromatography, let's have fun blending colors together to create new shades!

What you'll need:
- White paper or a drawing pad
- A variety of colored markers
- Water
- A paintbrush

Instructions:
- Take a white piece of paper or use a drawing pad as your canvas.
- Select two or more colored markers that you'd like to blend together to create new colors.
- Using the markers, draw small patches of each color on the paper, leaving some space between them.
- Dip a clean paintbrush into water and gently blend the colors where they meet. Watch as the pigments mix and create fantastic new colors!
- Experiment with different color combinations to see what colors you can create. You're now an artist who can mix pigments like a pro! Colors and pigments open up a world of creativity and wonder. Through chromatography, we've explored how colors can separate and create beautiful art pieces. We've also learned the art of blending pigments to create entirely new shades. The world of colors awaits your imaginative touch. Happy chromatography art!

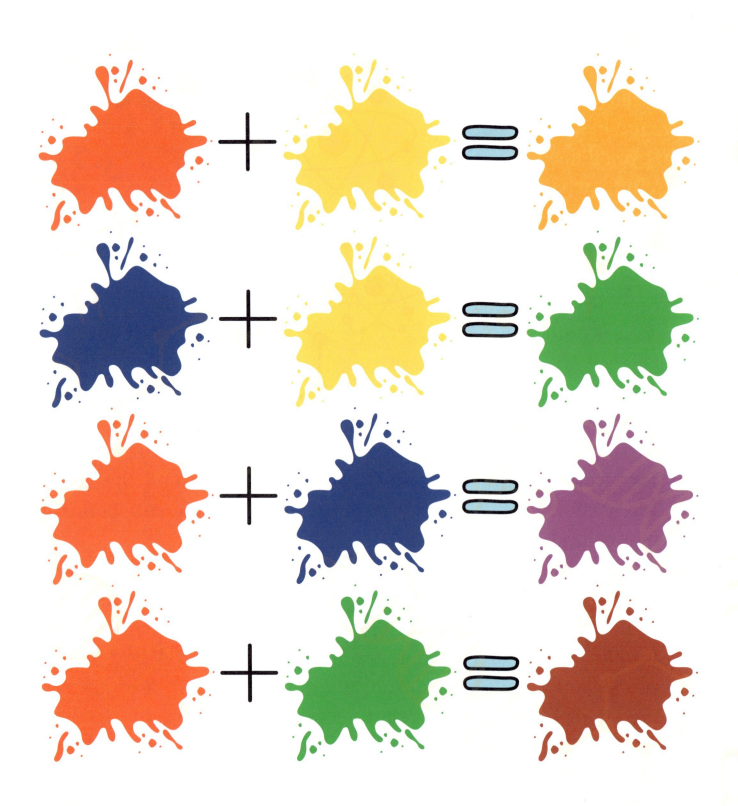

Rainbow Density Column

Welcome to a colorful and experiment that will leave you in awe! Today, we're going to create a magical rainbow right inside a glass using a simple but fascinating concept called density. As we journey through this experiment, you'll witness the science of layering different liquids to form a captivating and vibrant display that seems like it's straight out of a fairytale!

Materials You'll Need:
- A clear glass or a tall transparent container
- Honey or corn syrup
- Dishwashing liquid or colored water (with food coloring)
- Vegetable oil
- Cleaning alcohol (or rubbing alcohol)
- Water
- A spoon or dropper

Instructions:
- Gently pour a layer of honey, followed by corn syrup into the clear glass. See how they sparkle like golden treasure!
- Now, with a careful touch, add a layer of dishwashing liquid or colored water on top of the honey. Choose different colors to make your rainbow more eye-catching!
- Slowly pour a layer of vegetable oil onto the dishwashing liquid followed by water. Watch as it creates a shining layer!
- Finally, complete your rainbow by pouring a layer of vegetable oil, followed by cleaning alcohol on top. Behold the beauty and translucence finishing touch!

The Science Behind: What makes this rainbow-in-a-glass possible is a fascinating concept called density. Density is a property of matter that tells us how much mass a substance has in a given volume.

Alchocol
Vegetable Oil
Water
Dishwashing Liquid
Corn Syrup
Honey

Each liquid we used in this experiment has a different density, which is why they form separate layers instead of mixing together. Honey and corn syrup, being dense and heavy, settles at the bottom, serving as the foundation of our rainbow. On top of that, the dishwashing liquid and water, with their lesser densities, creates a striking contrast. The vegetable oil, with its own unique density, adds a shining layer to the display. And finally, the lighter cleaning alcohol graces the top with its ethereal presence.

Density In Everyday Life

Density is more than just a captivating concept in our rainbow. It's a fundamental aspect of everyday life! Think about why certain objects sink or float in water, or why oil separates from water when cooking. Density helps us understand these things.

For instance, when you put a piece of fruit in a bowl of water, it floats if its density is less than that of water. However, if it's denser than water, it sinks. Density also plays a role in the manufacturing of various products, from making food ingredients to constructing buildings and vehicles.

So, as you admire the intriguing rainbow density column, remember that this simple concept has a profound impact on the world around us!

Now, it's your turn to create your rainbow density column. Unleash your creativity and marvel at the wonders of science right in your glass!

Glossary Of Key Chemistry Terms

Chemistry is a fascinating world filled with unique terms and concepts. To help you better understand the world of chemistry, here's a simple glossary of key terms you encountered in this book and then some:

Chemistry Made Simple: Fun Words To Know

- Atom: The tiny building block of everything, atoms are made up of protons, neutrons, and electrons.
- Molecule: A group of atoms hanging out together, like best friends, to create something new.
- Element: A special substance that's found only in one flavor on the supercool periodic table.
- Periodic Table: A special table that organizes all the elements based on their unique features and behavior.
- Chemical Reaction: When substances and elements have a big party and change into brand new substances with new powers.
- Acid: A character who loves to share hydrogen, and their pH level is less than 7.
- Base: A character who loves to welcome hydrogen, and their pH level is more than 7.
- pH: A way to measure how things taste, if they are sour or sweet, or something in between.
- Matter: Everything that has weight and takes up space, like toys, water, and even air.
- Compound: A cool mix of different elements holding hands and sticking together.

- Solution: When one thing dissolves into another, like sugar happily disappearing in water.
- Chemical Bond: The superpower that keeps atoms together in a molecule, like glue for tiny particles.
- Density: How much stuff is packed into a space. It's like how many friends can fit in a tiny room!
- Evaporation: When liquids become so warm that they turn into invisible vapor and fly away.
- Condensation: When vapor gets chilly and turns back into droplets, like morning dew on grass.
- Physical Change: When something gets a makeover, but it's still the same on the inside, like when ice melts into water.
- Chemical Change: When a magical transformation happens, and something completely new appears just like when ash is produced from burning paper.
- Catalyst: A helper who speeds up cool reactions but doesn't join the party permanently, kind of like a DJ.
- Oxidation: When things hang out with oxygen and change their appearance, like rust on metal.
- Endothermic: Reactions that love to give hugs and take heat from the surroundings.
- Exothermic: Reactions that love to share warmth and give it to their surroundings.
- Alchemists: Alchemists were like magical scientists from long ago. They were curious and clever people who tried to unlock the secrets of the universe. Instead of using modern lab equipment, they had cauldrons and mysterious tools in their potions labs. Alchemists wanted to turn ordinary metals into valuable gold and find a magic potion called the "Philosopher's Stone" that could make them immortal.

- Though they didn't succeed in these quests, their passion for exploring the world and discovering new things laid the foundation for modern chemistry and science. Today, we remember them as adventurous dreamers who ignited the spark of curiosity in the world of science.

- Alchemy: Alchemy is like a magical and ancient science where people used to mix and experiment with different things to try to turn ordinary stuff into something special, like turning metals into gold or finding a magical elixir that grants eternal life. It's a bit like a fun and mysterious potion-making adventure, where people dreamed of unlocking the secrets of the universe and creating powerful and magical things!

- Ethereal: "Ethereal" is a word that describes something that feels like it's from a dream or a fairy tale. It's so beautiful and delicate that it seems to belong to a magical world. Imagine fluffy clouds that glow with a soft light or a shining, graceful butterfly floating through the air. That's what "ethereal" means - something that's so beautiful and almost too lovely to be real!

Epilogue: The Journey Ahead

Congratulations, young chemists, on completing this exciting journey through the world of chemistry! You have embarked on an extraordinary adventure, where you learned about the power of matter, reactions, and the beauty of the elements. As we draw near the end of this book, let us pause to reflect on the wonderful discoveries you have made and the fascinating path that lies ahead.

Exploring The Wonders of Chemistry

In these pages, you have discovered that chemistry is not just a subject in textbooks or laboratories; it is a language that whispers secrets about the universe. From the tiniest atoms to the grandest chemical reactions, you have seen how everything around us is composed of building blocks, creating a mesmerizing mosaic of matter. But this is only the beginning! The world of chemistry is vast and boundless.

Every day, scientists and researchers uncover new mysteries, delving deeper into the unknown. As you continue your exploration, you will witness astonishing breakthroughs that can change the way we live, heal, and understand our world.

One of the most crucial tools you carry with you on this journey is curiosity. Curiosity is the spark that ignites the flames of discovery. It is the driving force behind asking questions, seeking answers, and challenging the status quo. Embrace your curiosity, for it will lead you to astonishing places.

Keep asking "why" and "how." Don't be afraid to wonder and ponder, even about the simplest things. Curiosity knows no boundaries, and it is by embracing this spirit of inquiry that you will unravel some of the most profound mysteries of our existence.

As you step forward, remember that you, young readers, hold the potential to become the scientists and explorers of tomorrow. Your ideas, your enthusiasm, and your willingness to question can shape the future of chemistry and the world at large.

Seek knowledge beyond the classroom, as the world is your laboratory, waiting for your keen observations and brilliant experiments. From the kitchen to the garden, from the stars above to the oceans below, chemistry is everywhere. Discover it in the vibrant colors of a sunset, the scent of blooming flowers, and the taste of your favorite foods.

With your newfound knowledge of chemistry, a world of opportunities awaits you. You may choose to pursue a career in science and delve deeper into the complexities of matter. Or perhaps you will apply your understanding of chemistry to create innovative solutions to global challenges, such as sustainable energy or environmental protection.

But regardless of the path you choose, always carry the spirit of curiosity in your heart. It will continue to lead you toward new horizons and fuel your passion for exploration. As we conclude this journey through the wonders of chemistry, remember that the pursuit of knowledge is a never-ending expedition. So, my young chemists, stay curious! Embrace the unknown, celebrate the joy of discovery, and always seek to expand your understanding of the world. Just as atoms bond together to create molecules, knowledge and curiosity combine to

Spark a revolution of understanding. So, take this book as a stepping stone on your expedition through the realm of chemistry. There is so much more to explore, to learn, and to celebrate. Embrace the wonders of chemistry, and let your curiosity guide you to a future filled with endless possibilities.

Remember, young chemists, the journey has just begun! Stay curious, and the world will reveal its mysteries to you.

With heartfelt congratulations and best wishes,

DAVID SOUGHTOUT

P.S. To all the young scientists out there, thank you for joining me on this Journey! There's more to come! Keep your eyes peeled for Volume 2, where we'll explore even more exciting experiments and mysteries together. Until then, keep exploring, keep dreaming, and keep your love for science alive! See you in there.

Made in the USA
Columbia, SC
09 June 2025